" I can't brag about how I love God because I fail Him daily. But I can brag about His love for us because it never fails."

Dedication

These stories are dedicated to the staff of Kokomo Urban Outreach; they have been amazing throughout all of these disasters. Thank you: John, Pam, Deanna, Sue, Avery and Ricky. Without the support of the community, churches, organizations, and individuals, KUO would not be able to meet the challenges. Thank you for your support. Special thanks to my wife Chris along with my entire family.

Introduction

Kokomo has seen its fair share of disasters the past few years: financial downturn, a flood, and a tornado. It has been difficult. It has always been about neighbors helping neighbors. When the TV shows "Extreme Home Makeover" and "Restaurant Impossible" were here, they both said they had never had so many volunteers to help.

When the floods came in April of 2013, people were out helping neighbors salvage personal belongings. When the tornadoes came seven months later, the community helped again. Hopefully, these stories will provide inspiration and perhaps healing, for all were affected and helped during these disasters.

These stories are told through the eyes of Kokomo Urban Outreach. Other organizations have different stories to share and I am anxious to hear them. This little book does not tell every story; they are inspirational stories, stories of hope and unconditional love. There is still so much work to be done, homes to rebuild, businesses to re-open, and families to be restored. As that work continues throughout the coming months, let us continue to be in prayer for our leaders and those working in the recovery effort. We have a long way to go, but I can't help believing God is up to something! **To God be the Glory!!!!**

Part One

By the Waters By Lyne Stull-Lipps. .

(Inspired by Psalm 137)

By the waters of the creek we sit and weep as we
remembered our homes.

Having lost our furniture, our clothing , our family pictures,
our journals where we recorded the stories of our lives...
we huddle together waiting for help to arrive.

Our rescuers ask us to be patient, help is on its way,
sing a song to bide the time.

But how can we sing songs, when all we have,
our past and our future, is buried in the deluge?

Let our hearts sorrow... in time they will be healed.

We will remember our cities;
we will honor our towns;
we will rebuild our neighborhoods.

And one day, when the crisis has passed,
we will tell again the stories,
and play once more the music of our city.

The Church has left the Building!

As the floodwaters receded, families began to return home to start cleaning-up. One mother wept when she realized that all her family's clothes were ruined. Travis Taflinger, one of the co-founders of Bridges Outreach, lived only one block from the destruction. As the snow fell after the flood, he began to help to his neighbors. He made a few phone calls to local church pastors, and soon scores of people began to flood into neighborhoods to help salvage the unsalvageable. The Church had left their buildings!

The rain came on Thursday, waters crested on Friday, and the church began its work on Saturday. After talking with Travis and the staff at Kokomo Urban Outreach (KUO), it became apparent that there was a need to collect clothing, furniture, appliances, and cleaning supplies and then distribute them to those in need. Travis listened to the neighbors' needs, and we responded. Travis was able to secure a warehouse and Deanna Ancil from KUO was selected to staff it.

In response to the articulated need, we announced on Monday, just three days after the water crested, that KUO would begin collecting items for flood-affected families. Tuesday morning items began arriving, and by noon items were going out. The warehouse was opened for six weeks, moving furniture to new homes, giving clothing to children so they could return to school, and providing bleach, flood buckets and other clean up items. Huge amounts of items came in and went out. God listened to neighbors' cries for help, Travis listened to God and expressed the need, and the community responded—big time. **God is good!**

Mattress Day

Ann had trouble getting up that morning. It was her first night of sleeping on the floor. She had been staying at the shelter that had closed the day before. Ann had nowhere to go except back to her home. Her furniture was piled on the side of the street. She had nowhere to sleep but on the floor, and at her age she had trouble getting up.

Van Taylor, the Executive Director of the Kokomo Rescue Mission, had some mattresses that were donated by a local motel. Travis shared the need of mattresses, Van offered them, and off we went. Van, Travis, myself and some staff went door to door listening to stories, praying with folks and giving them mattresses. It was as if we were "Publishers Clearing House" presenting each family with a check; the mattresses were like gold. When asked where the mattresses came from, we simply said God gave them to the Rescue Mission and the Mission gave them to you. That day everyone who was home took some mattresses. Need heard, need met, **praise God!**

We are Weak, but He is Strong

A woman confined to a hospital bed in her living room survived the flood by holding her head above the water as it slowly rose around her body. She was taken to the hospital, and the dirty flood water entered her body, causing an infection. Her bed was destroyed and she had nowhere to sleep. In less than a day her bed was replaced by Homeland Security. When she was released from the hospital, she moved in with family members.

A 92-year-old man was reluctant to leave his rented house and all of his belongings. The flood waters had receded several days earlier. He felt he was safe. However, there was mold growing on walls and on his tile floor. With no family in the area, he was finally convinced by Officer Jim Gunlight to go to a motel where he stayed until a niece from Pennsylvania took him home with her. While he escaped with his life, he lost everything. Food was taken to him each day while he stayed in the motel and he received new clothes from the warehouse.

We received a thank you note from his niece saying, "The first thing we did when we got to PA was get him to a doctor. We caught his pneumonia just in time. He is doing much better. He wants his own place but we agree it is best for him to stay here with us for now. We had no idea how bad his house was. He is very precious to all of us and he will be well taken care of. Again thank you to Kokomo Urban Outreach and Officer Gunlight for caring for him."

These stories remind me of a childhood song:

Jesus loves me! This I know, For the Bible tells me so;
Little ones to Him belong;
They are weak, but He is strong.
Yes, Jesus loves me.......

No Pants, No School

I saw them walk in: a tall man with holes in his jeans, a woman who was wearing clothing that looked uncomfortably tight, and an 11-year-old boy holding the side of his pants to keep them from falling down. I introduced myself and asked them how we could help. I soon learned that they were family who had lost everything. They needed clothing. All they had was what they were wearing.

The father told me he lost his job in the recession, along with their house and car. The father seemed defeated as he spoke. He shared that he had to move his family into the "hole" because that was all he could afford. He had lived there just a few months and said, "What the recession didn't take, the flood did."

I told him that he did not live in the "hole"; he lived in a home that flooded. The "hole" is a derogatory name for a flood prone neighborhood that has repeatedly flooded. Others call it the "fishbowl," as it is underwater more than any other place in the city. Many of the houses were rentals that low income families could afford. They aren't the nicest houses in town, but it was a roof over a family. Since the flood, the city has purchased the houses in the "hole" and are currently razing them. ***That is God at work.*** Houses that would have been nearly impossible to sell, sold. What a deal. For now, the area will be green space that will border an existing walking trail.

The father looked down, somewhat embarrassed and told me his son hasn't been able to go to school because he did not have any pants to wear. The father showed me how the boy was wearing his pants and without a belt the boy was doing his best to hold them up. The pants were way too long and too big around, and it was obvious that the boy was self-conscience of the predicament he was in.

I invited the family to pick out as many clothes as they wanted and encouraged them to get their son to school that day. He needed "normalcy," and he needed it now.

We were able to find his family a new place to live. Because of the generosity of the people of Kokomo, this family's new house was completely furnished. Today the father is working two jobs and the mother has a part-time job. **God is in the business of restoring families!**

Amazing Grace

During the early days following the flood, I attended meeting after meeting with other community leaders, discussing how we were going to respond and recover from the flood. It seemed like things were moving very slowly. United Methodist leaders in the state of Indiana called and asked how they could help. We talked about the need to get drywall out and drywall up, and I explained that people need hot water heaters and, by fall, furnaces. Within one day of the conversation, KUO received a check from the United Methodist Church for $60,000. We had already received about $10,000 from the community. The $60,000 went a long way in providing families with furnaces, hot water heaters, mold mitigation and drywall repair. The Red Cross had been helping families with first month's rent and deposits, helping families relocate. Many families could not relocate before the Red Cross deadline for helping expired. The $10,000 was used for deposits, helping to relocate people after the Red Cross left.

The Center Township Trustee, Jean Lushin, provided families with stoves and refrigerators. The Trustee's office also provided volunteers to work the recovery warehouse. The Kokomo Rescue Mission provided "staff and trucks" to move things from the warehouse to homes. The Salvation Army provided the warehouse with mattresses and cleaning supplies. When the work of the warehouse was completed, nearly all needs had been met.

Families were thankful for the unconditional love that was given to them. One person said, "At first we had help from the Red Cross and after a couple of weeks I felt lost, but now I feel like I have been found. I have a place to live, furniture, clothing, food and new appliances. Thank you!" In his words, I lived "Amazing Grace": I was lost but now am found. ***God is amazing!***

Work Teams from Where?

I received an email from a pastor in Huntington Beach, California. He wanted to bring his youth group to Kokomo to help with the flood recovery. I thought, "Wow, that's a long way". They were going to fly to Indianapolis, rent vans, sleep on church floors and give a week. Not long after, I received phone calls from a church in Mooresville, Indiana; Medina, Ohio; Flint, Michigan; and finally, Elkhart, Indiana. What they all had in common was they were youth who wanted to serve. Most stayed for a week. When they arrived, they shared stories of how they raised funds to come to Kokomo, a city most of them had never heard of before. However, their parents had heard of the Beach Boys and shared the song "Kokomo" with their kids (that song was played a bit too much, for me, while they were here, but they liked it). While they came to work they also learned about Kokomo, the city I love. They all went to Kokomo Beach, they enjoyed the parks, some visited the museums, and they were impressed with the beauty of downtown. They rode the trolleys and ate some local food—few had experienced a giant breaded tenderloin, and none had ever had a baked hamburger from Coney Island. The biggest surprise was the group from California, who thought White Castle was a fictional restaurant in a movie. When they found out it was real—they ate a lot.

The work teams came to work, and work they did. Under the leadership of Rev. Dale Bliss and Rev. Lee Miller construction was planned and executed. By the time the teams had left, the majority of the construction work was completed. The last team, from Ohio, hosted a dinner at Trinity United Methodist Church for the families whom they helped. Residents shared how grateful they were for the teams restoring homes. Lots of tears were shed that night.

"Prayer in action is love, and love in action is service. Try to give unconditionally whatever a person needs in the moment. The point is to do something, however small, and show you care through your actions by giving your time ... We are all God's children so it is important to share His gifts. Do not worry about why problems exist in the world – just respond to people's needs ... We feel what we are doing is just a drop in the ocean, but that ocean would be less without that drop."- Mother Teresa

Rock and Roll

When the last work team left, at the end of July, almost everything was done. Dale and his team were finishing odds and ends. Then it got cold, and furnaces that were thought to work didn't. Soon we were installing furnaces all over the place, and it was a good thing there was still money left from the United Methodist gift. It was at this time I met Abby.

Abby has an incredible story. Abby is a young librarian, who doesn't look like your stereotypical librarian: she is tattooed and a collector of rock and roll memorabilia.

As water seeped into her house, her father came with a boat, to save her rock and roll collection. Trip after trip from boat to truck and back, and many of her belongings were saved.

Things were looking good for Abby. She received a grant from Homeland Security; she purchased a furnace, hot water heater, breaker box, drywall, and they made a plan to move walls, to raise the roof in the back, to remodel the kitchen, and to build a loft to store her rock 'n roll collection. Her modest house was being transformed into a dream house.

Then tragedy struck again: her father was killed in a traffic accident. However, Amy was determined to see their plans completed. While a recovery grant would not allow us to remodel by adding a loft, raising a roof, or moving a wall, I was able to promise that when that work was done, we could do the wiring, install flooring, put up drywall, and finish the plumbing. When I spoke to her August, and it seemed like a lot for her to get done on her own , I told her we could put it back the way it was originally. She graciously declined and was determined to see her father's and her dream realized. I asked her to call me when it was done, and we could help with drywall, wiring etc. To be honest, I didn't think I would hear from her again. She called last week, right after the tornado hit. She said she was just about done and asked whether the offer still stood to help her finish. My answer: "Of course it does."

It appears that when Abby's house is complete, the flood recovery will be complete. Which will be perfect, as all of our money for flood recovery will be gone. **God is an amazing provider!**

Part Two

A hymn by Charles Tindley 1901

When the storms of life are raging, Stand by me.
When the storms of life are raging, Stand by me;
When the world is tossing me; Like a ship upon the sea
Thou Who rulest wind and water, Stand by me.

In the midst of tribulation, Stand by me;
In the midst of tribulation, Stand by me;
When the hosts of hell assail, And my strength begins to fail,
Thou Who never lost a battle, Stand by me.

Tindley was a pastor of a Methodist Church in the early 1900's. He worked with business leaders to assist his members in finding jobs. He also encouraged members to start their own businesses and purchase homes. The church formed the East Calvary Building and Loan Association to offer mortgages. Tindley also solicited donations of food from businessmen for the congregation's ministry of feeding the needy.

Tindley objected to social events that he considered degrading, including the 1912 Cake Walk and Ball, and The Soap Box Minstrels show at the Academy of Music on Broad and Locust Streets. Tindley always stood with the oppressed and weathered many storms. ***In the midst of the Kokomo Storms we know who is standing beside us and helping us to move forward....God.***

Not Again

The weather report for that day said, "60% chance of Tornados", I have never heard a percentage attached to a tornado. It was Sunday, and the food was already done for the "Neighborhood of Hope" dinner. Something just didn't feel right to me so called Deanna and we decided to cancel the meals. Deanna began making phone calls—a lot of phone calls. It is hard to cancel meals in multiple neighborhoods on a Sunday afternoon.

I, on the other hand, went to a funeral visitation, followed by a church meeting and then a church rally. I left after the church meeting and returned home. I was home alone. The sky was dark and just as I went into the house, rain came pouring down. The lights flickered and I tried to find the dog to go to the basement. As I picked her up it sounded like big hail stones hitting the house. I ran to a hallway and braced myself. The house began to shake and I could hear windows breaking, along with "the sound" everyone says they hear when in a tornado. It really just lasted a couple of minutes, not long at all. I opened my front door and went on the porch; it looked like a bomb had gone off across the street, yet it was eerily quiet. Neighbors were running up and down the street checking on each other. My neighbors in the housing complex across the street were trying to stop traffic from going down Hoffer Street as trees and power lines were down. There was the second floor of a house sitting in the middle of Home Ave. I watched as people started climbing out the window and began to pray. The quiet turned to sirens and help was on the way.

Over the course of the evening I learned that several areas of the city had been hit: on Hoffer St. from Home to 31, businesses and homes damaged or destroyed; in the Maple Crest area, Cedar Crest and Bell/Rickets and several other neighborhoods were damaged.

Travis Taflinger came to my office on Monday morning. He had been put in charge of the volunteer relief effort. Travis is recognized in the community as the "Get-it-Done Guy"—he is very connected to the community, he has integrity, and people respond to him. Travis came to our office on Monday and made call after call, planning, organizing, and working to get clean up started. Some areas were hit so hard that no one was allowed to go in. Travis honed in to the Hoffer St. area for clean up. That morning he had the Crossings School cleaning up yards, removing debris, and helping with general clean-up in the neighborhood. A little after noon, Casey Cline (co-founder with Travis at Bridges Outreach) came leading a group of over 250 high school students who gave up their "day off" of school to help their neighbors. Officer Gunlight secured a dumpster; it was filled quickly, and by mid-afternoon a second one was delivered. By the end of the day our immediate neighborhood was clean. Travis continued to work through the evening, planning for the next day. Travis moved volunteers all around the city, chainsaws roaring, to clear debris , facilitating clean-up. Within ten days, hundreds of volunteers had made a difference. Travis and his crew knew how to get it done!

Send in the Pros

Children started filtering into the Outreach's home base, Trinity United Methodist Church. They visit us often especially when school is out. Right across the street from the church is government housing, Garden Square (also known as Gateway). The children know the church is a safe place, a place where they can talk freely, and for many it is a second home. It was apparent that many children were suffering emotionally. The apartments were not directly hit, but hearts were hit. Many children told stories of hiding in closets, under beds, or in the bathtub. They could hear it, coming; they shared how whole families screamed and cried. When it was over, they went outside and saw utter destruction across the street—horrible sights. Then came a night with no power, no lights, no heat, and no way to cook. We could tell they had been traumatized.

On Monday there was no school. The Outreach had lunch for the neighbors, and about 200 were served. An email was sent out for help, and the response was amazing. People were coming in to cook and serve, others were coming in to volunteer to clean up outside, still others were answering the phone for our staff so that we could supervise the volunteers. I had been outside helping, before going to check out the dining room. I walked by Mrs. Campbell, the principal of

Elwood Haynes school, then looked around the room, and what I saw brought tears to my eyes. The neighborhood children's teachers had come to eat lunch with them, reassuring them that things would return to normal soon. The crisis counselor for the school corporation was there, as well as the food service director, all pitching in to help. The children were feeling a bit more secure by afternoon. Many began helping pick up shingles in the yards.

That night at dinner, the folks from the Housing Authority were there to help serve, including Deputy Director Jeff Kearns and Resident Liaison Joe Millan. We were so crowded that I was washing dishes with an Indy Crash Football Player (women's professional football) and Jeff Kearns kept shaking the water off the trays and running them back out to the serving lines.

It was great to have the "pros" with us on the first day---quietly, humbly serving. ***Isn't it just like God to think of everything?***

KUO Staff

"Emergency staff meeting Monday morning 9:00 AM sharp" was the text I sent out Sunday Night to my staff. Deanna Ancil is the Director of Operations , John Martin is the Director of Food Security, Sue Bond is the Director of Family Advocacy, Pam Grohman is the Assistant to the Executive Director, Avery is Facilities Manager, and Ricky is an intern through the K-serve program. All the staff received specific jobs that day.

Sue would oversee outside volunteers, Deanna would oversee inside volunteers, John and Ricky would run the food pantry for the day, and Pam would plan for evening activities. Our plan was to provide breakfast, lunch, and dinner with a warm place to hang out until the power returned to Garden Square. Evening activities included games and a movie, along with homework help, until 8:00 PM. Then the children were taken home to go to bed. The KUO staff are all part-time folks, but they put in an incredible amount of time the first week, all while keeping the usual activities of the Outreach going. We still had all pantries open, and we had a clothing giveaway, as well as extra phone calls. At the same time, we were planning to have 2000 people over for Thanksgiving Dinner. The KUO staff kept the pace. We felt the prayers for us; we appreciate it and still need it. The KUO staff has diverse personalities, gifts and skills, yet we all work well together . . . just like the Bible says: ***"Many parts, one body."***

Beanie Babies

During the week after the tornado, many people brought us things they thought we could use. As we were going through bags of donations, we found a bag of Beanie Babies and inside this handwritten note was found:

When I was seven, my house got destroyed by a tornado. I remember being carried out of the wreckage and seeing my house now a pile of sticks on the ground. And in those few seconds this tornado took my house, it had taken much more from me. It took my safety. I didn't know I could recover or that my safety would return. Thankfully, we were taking care of by our friends, family, my parents work and complete strangers. The next couple of weeks were very difficult as I tried to grasp the situation. Suddenly, I was looking in apartments on the other side of town with nothing (Praise God) except my family. One day I remember getting a bag of Beanie Babies from one of my mom's friends. After staring at them in awe, I realized that life could, and would, get back to normal.

Over the past 15 years, I have been collecting stuffed animals. I could never bring myself to give them away or donate them. I never knew why until last night (11/17/13). I could not fall asleep. I kept thinking of all the pictures of damaged and destroyed houses I'd seen throughout the day. I couldn't help but see my destroyed house in these pictures. I realized in this moment I have been collecting these stuffed animals all these years for this very moment.

I pray that these contributions will go to the children who need them and they will give those children hope that one day they will get back to their normal life and that they will feel safe again. Thank you.

The note was unsigned but from the note we know she is 22 years old and is *paying it forward* and is helping children find normalcy. ***God restores our lives.***

The Miracle of the Poles

By Wednesday, all of our neighbors' refrigerator and freezer food had to be discarded—that was traumatic. Many folks are "food insecure" already; wasted food is not an option for most. The newspaper provided a glimmer of hope when it reported that the power throughout the whole county would be back on by noon on Wednesday. I was told on Tuesday that Garden Square's power would be later than that, due to destroyed power poles and not enough poles to go around. I was told it would be at least Friday if not into the following week. It was like a punch in the gut to our neighbors when we told them that the power would not come on with everyone else's.

Our neighbors, in the apartments, lack all kinds of resources: financial support, family support, and all kinds of safety nets. Some in the community expected "those" families to go to a shelter, and some of them did. However, many didn't. Most families wanted to stay to protect their belongings from looters, to put their children on the bus at the normal time and place, and just be at home. Few have cars, so running from a shelter back home to pick up a few things wasn't possible. As I talked with many, they stated they stayed to support one another; one reminded me of the images of the shelters in Katrina, saying she didn't want to be part of that. Most value privacy. For whatever reason, some of our neighbors chose to stay close.

“Just hold tight” was the mantra for Wednesday, trying to be encouragers yet knowing that there would be no power on that day. Then the miraculous: there were utility workers in the neighborhood at about 10:00 AM. Suddenly, where there were no power poles to be had, out of nowhere power poles were found. Crews worked all day.

At dinner that night, about 100 people were sitting at tables waiting to eat, and we received word that the power just came back on. I walked into the dining room and made the big announcement. There were shouts of joy and clapping with a party breaking out. It wasn’t just a celebration of power returning: it was a victory celebration of beating the storm. They did it, they really did it. They stayed, and they made it. Amazing. I will always remember November 20 as “The Miracle of the Poles” Day.

When things calmed down, the diners were asked who would like to pray for the meal. A little 7-year-old raised his hand. The room got very quiet and the boy prayed, ***"God, thank you for helping us to help each other. . ."***

DNA

Right before our epic Thanksgiving Dinner, a TV news reporter showed up at the church. Being on the news is OK as it tells the story, but it is not something I enjoy. The reporter asked me a bunch of questions, but one ruffled my feathers. He asked, “What surprised you the most about the way Kokomo came together to help each other? This was pretty unusual right?" I was polite and responded, "Nothing surprised me!" When I looked at him I could see a question mark on his face. I repeated it again: "Nothing." I went on to tell him that I was born, raised, and have lived most of my life in Kokomo. I told him that like any other city, we are full of people with different views on different issues. I also told him that most of us are pretty adamant in our views, with most not afraid to express them. I told him that not everyone gets along with each other; however, we have been told Kokomo is different. Hen Extreme Home Makeover and Restaurant Impossible came to town, and both television shows reported they had never, ever, anywhere else had so many people come out to help. Just say, "We Care," to see how Kokomo responds. Folks have fundraiser to buy wheelchairs, buy medicine, or meet any unmet need a family truly has. Kokomo pride happens when everyone pitches in to help. I told him about the flood in April, along with a list of other disasters, and I explained that this is Kokomo after all. Helping our neighbors is in our DNA, and there is nothing anyone can do to destroy that. I told him that folks from all backgrounds roll up their sleeves and get the job done. I also said to him, "When we help, we help, everyone. In a disaster there are no Democrats or Republicans. No one cares how you voted, the color of your skin, whether you are gay or straight, or whether you are a Methodist, Baptist, Pentecostal or none of the above. We are all just people helping people, neighbors helping neighbors, friends helping friends. ***We can't help it—it is in our DNA.***

Thanksgiving Dinner

In the midst of helping our neighbors ride out the power outrage, one of our biggest events, Thanksgiving dinner, was fast approaching. When I returned to Kokomo in 2005, Bob Cox, the then director of the Kokomo Rescue Mission, asked me why few people from Garden Square came to downtown to Thanksgiving Dinner. I reminded him that was far to walk, since few of my neighbors have transportation. He responded by saying, "Can we bring Thanksgiving Dinner to you?" He suggested the night before Thanksgiving, as the Mission would be serving downtown on Thanksgiving Day. I was way open to that. KUO's first Thanksgiving Dinner took place 6 weeks before KUO was officially birthed, and nearly 200 people came to the first dinner. At the first dinner I thought it would be nice to put table cloths on the tables—real ones, with decorations. Then I thought real plates not paper, no serving line, restaurant style: we would serve our neighbors and we would do it right. Morning Star Church came to help serve and do dishes. When one of the guys finished the dishes, he asked me, "Why real plates, why not paper?" My response was, "Don't the poor deserve real plates on Thanksgiving?" Conversation over. When I see this man, he often reminds me I "messed him up", with that comment. I know people in poverty have issues and aren't perfect. However, they often have no voice, and one of my goals for KUO is to give a voice to the poor.

This year was our 9th Wednesday Night Thanksgiving Meal.

After all of these years we still partner with the Kokomo Rescue Mission; my friend Van Taylor is now the executive director. Morning Star Church still sends people to help at Trinity, and people are still served a great meal. However, it is different, really different. We serve in meals all across the city (15 locations) to nearly 2,000 people. This year was different too, as everyone had a great deal to be thankful for—you could see it all over their faces. ***Thank God!***

Hope^2

The last thing we need is to have this disaster cause another disaster. We don't want people without jobs, without food, or without spiritual health. So, where do we go from here?

There will be a long-term recovery committee that will help families who lost homes rebuild. KUO will ***not*** be a part of the group, as we are still helping flood recovery. We are close to being done with flood recovery but not quite.

My concern is stabilizing families while offering hope. I am calling this intuitive Hope "Squared" which will address two things:

1. Provide basic needs not just to families whose houses were affected by the tornado, but will include those whose lives were affected. There are many people who lost their jobs, due to destroyed businesses. They have shelter but not the basic needs. We are trying to fill our pantries with food and hygiene supplies to help these families. We are

sure that in the next few weeks and into the New Year the needs will be great. You can help by providing food and hygiene items.

2. Provide emotional and spiritual help to those who desire it. I am putting together a network of pastors and counselors to work with families who are struggling with trauma. Everyone needs someone in the midst of a crisis.

Hope[2] is only about two things: basic needs and healing—neither costs much. We are not asking for money (so many have been generous in the past) to support the Outreach in this endeavor.

Hope[2] is not about throwing money at a problem, but for caring for and/or spending time with a family right here in your neighborhood.

Bragging about God

I received an email a few days before the tornado, from the Kokomo Huddle (the Huddle is a Christ-centered men's group which meets each Wednesday). It asked, "Do you ever brag about God?" That hit my heart, especially the week of the tornado relief effort. There was a great deal of bragging, that week, in the newspaper which included a couple of articles about Kokomo Urban Outreach. That's all fine and dandy, but we must never forget who is really working. I wrote this article on November 22, just five days after the tornado. Here goes:

Today I want to brag about God in the midst of the storm. As I was sitting in my house on Sunday, I heard the tornado coming, felt the house shaking, and heard the windows breaking; however, I was safe.

With no power in Garden Square, this meant no heat, no cooking, etc. Our staff prayed and in the prayer time we felt God was asking us to serve the less fortunate in our neighborhood, but how was another question. We prayed for food. God provided. Churches came out in droves to provide food for us to cook for our friends and neighbors.

We needed milk. . . 39 gallons came from a local church. God provided for His children.

We needed coffee, and within 10 minutes, 8 canisters of coffee came in from a church.

On Monday we received a call from a Christian Food Bank saying a semi with food was on its way. By 3:00 pm, less than 24 hours after the tornado, food was here to stock our pantries. There was $24,000 worth of food and supplies on the truck.

May I keep bragging about God? The debris in the neighborhood was huge and dangerous, with many kids out of school exploring the 2x4's and nails. How to clean it up to keep children safe? Prayer. And suddenly, scores of high school students came flocking down the alley, led by Joey Hurlocker, a pastor's son. He said, "God put it on my heart to call 40 friends to come help"—they were over 250 strong. By the end of Monday we were almost cleaned up. Every yard, every person.

Our staff saw signs of stress in the children; we needed help to bring them hope. Their teachers showed up out of the blue at lunch on Monday, sat with children, and reassured them. Isn't it just like God to send in the "pros"?

By Tuesday, a representative of the United Methodist Church provided us with $4,000 for food and $700 worth of flashlights for our neighbors. More and more volunteers arrived to serve.

Tuesday was a day of what I call "Loaves and Fishes." Prepared food poured in and by the end of Tuesday, God had provided our neighborhood with over 500 different volunteers, and nearly 600 stomachs filled, with lots of food left over.

Tuesday was also the day our neighbors realized their perishable food was gone. We continued to pray for guidance and God's help. Tuesday night we still weren't sure we knew what to do.

After we closed up at 8:00 PM, I went home to pray.

Wednesday morning it was reported in the newspaper that most of the power would be on by noon in Howard County. Except for Garden Square. Garden Square needed new power poles and all of the power poles were gone. We were told it could be Friday or maybe into Thanksgiving before power was restored. We prayed, "God the babies are cold. . . . help them." By 5:00 pm on Wednesday the power had been restored. God is Good!

Wednesday afternoon 7th graders from Acacia Academy finished cleaning up the neighborhood. Neighborhood clean with the help of neighbors and volunteers.

I'm not preaching here, but I am going to continue to brag about God. We began trusting in God that He would restore spoiled food to the food-insecure families, but how? There are about 200 apartments in Garden Square: nearly impossible. Suddenly, the Federal Government could put money back on food stamp cards to replace lost food. Here is the big miracle. . . . sign up on Thursday, money on card by Friday. Wow!!! God is good. The Housing Authority would shuttle neighbors back and forth to the store.

Those who do not receive food stamps would have food restored through the kindness of Meijer.

Now we are praying how we can help people in the long run. Many low-income workers lost pay checks due to lack of work at damaged businesses. How are they going to make it through December, January, and beyond? We expect our pantries will be very busy in the weeks ahead. We prayed on Monday for food pantry food to come through. In recent days, we have seen Facebook posts and Tweets about food drives this weekend that will benefit our community. Food is pouring into our Buckeye warehouse.

Over $65,000 has come through our office in the past several days to be used for food. God is taking care of us so that we can take care of others. I am sure you will not see any news articles bragging about what God has done, but at least you have seen it here.

All of this can be summed up by the prayer of a little 7-year-old boy who prayed before a meal: ""**God, thank you for helping us to help each other. . ." Thank you for being a vessel of God!!**

Jeff Newton 2013

Executive Director of Kokomo Urban Outreach

Flood April 2013

Little Boy waiting for Mom to find him some clothes at the KUO Flood Recovery Center

Standing on my front porch right after Tornado hit. Looking across Hoffer St.

www.ingramcontent.com/pod-product-compliance
Ingram Content Group UK Ltd.
Pitfield, Milton Keynes, MK11 3LW, UK
UKHW020227250726
13967UKWH00001B/229

9 781304 693853